VET

IN TRAINING

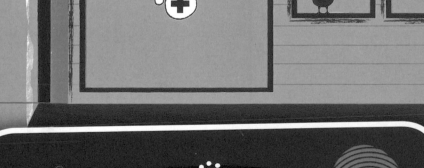

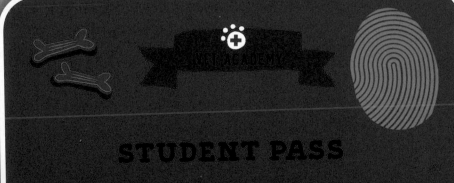

VET ACADEMY

STUDENT PASS

Name ....

 KINGFISHER

First published 2019 by Kingfisher
an imprint of Macmillan Children's Books
The Smithson. 6–9 Briset Street. London EC1M 5NR
Associated companies throughout the world
www.panmacmillan.com

Series editor: Kath Jewitt
Design: Jeni Child

ISBN 978-0-7534-4420-7

Copyright © Macmillan Publishers International Ltd 2019

9 8 7 6 5 4 3 2 1
1TR/0519/WKT/UG/128MA

A CIP catalogue record for this book is available from the British Library.

Printed in China

Picture credits
The Publisher would like to thank the following for permission to reproduce their material.
Top = t: Bottom = b: Centre = c: Left = l: Right = r
iStock: Proskuneo 18cb: olkim 18ct. Shutterstock: dashingstock 16bl: TJ Images 16br:
Vlad Siaber 17br: Christian Buch 17bl: HelloRF Zcool 22t.

VET
IN TRAINING

Can you find the chick on each page?

KINGFISHER

VET ACADEMY

TRAINING PROGRAMME

THEORY

THEORY pages are full of important information that you need to know.

PRACTICAL

PRACTICAL pages have a task to do for a vet skill to acquire. Tick each page when you have completed that part of your training.

TRAINING TIME

THEORY NO: 1
tick here
APPROVED

So you want to be a vet? Do you love all animals?
Are you good with people? Are you okay with goo and poo?
Then this could be the job for you!

WHAT'S THE JOB?

Vets look after all sorts of sick and injured animals.
They also make sure healthy animals don't get poorly.

Here are a few of the things that a vet has to do...

O See people and their animals
at the vets' surgery.

O Give out
medicines to
make sick
animals feel
better.

These pets have
all been to see the
vet. Can you spot
the odd one out?

6

○ Give advice to owners about the best way to care for their animals.

○ Carry out operations on poorly or injured animals.

MEET THE VETS!

Find out what vets say about their jobs.

<<I love making people's pets well. If the pets are very poorly it can be sad, too.>>

<<When I am 'on-call' I have to treat sick animals in the middle of the night.>>

<<Every day is different and I get to work with lots of amazing animals.>>

CAREER FINDER

What sort of vet job is right for you?
Find out by answering the questions and
following the trails on this career-finder map.

Then you should be...

AN EXOTIC PET VET

START HERE

 Do you like animals that look cute and cuddly?

NO

Are you into creatures that creep, crawl and slither?

NO

YES

YES

Do you like danger and adventure?

YES

Do you prefer dry land to life at sea?

NO

NO

YES

Then you should be...

A SMALL ANIMAL VET

Then you should be...

A WILDLIFE VET

Then you should be...

AN EQUINE VET

Then you should be...

A FARM VET

YES

YES

SMALL ANIMAL VETS: work in a surgery looking after pets, such as cats, dogs and hamsters.

WILDLIFE VETS: work in safari parks and rescue centres. They treat wild animals, such as lions, tigers and apes.

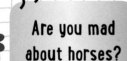

Are you mad about horses?

NO

Do you like being outside whatever the weather?

EXOTIC PET VETS: work in a surgery caring for unusual pets, such as spiders, snakes and lizards.

NO

EQUINE VETS: travel to farms, ranches and stables to treat horses and ponies.

Then you should be...

AN AQUATIC VET

FARM VETS: travel from farm to farm, looking after cows, sheep and pigs.

Read this book and then...

COME BACK AND TRY AGAIN!

AQUATIC VETS: work in aquariums and marine parks. They treat fish, turtles, seals and other sea creatures.

THEORY NO: 2
tick here
APPROVED

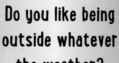
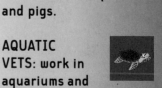

ANIMAL BODIES

Vets' patients come in all shapes and sizes, but under the fur, feathers and scales, many animals are not so different.

X-RAY EXAMINATION

Humans and animals have a lot of the same kinds of bones.

Can you spot these bones on the dog's skeleton?

O skull
O ribs
O vertebrae bones

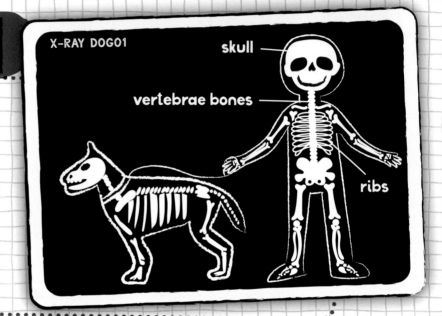

X-RAY DOG01

skull

vertebrae bones

ribs

ARMS, FLIPPERS AND WINGS

a)

b)

c)

d)

Animal 'arm' bones are shaped differently to help them grab, swim, leap or fly.

Can you match each animal to its arm, wing or flipper?

Bat

Whale

Monkey

Frog

10

ADAPTABLE ANIMALS

Although some human and animal skeletons can be quite alike, some animals are very different, too.

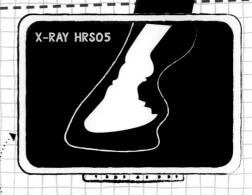
X-RAY HRS05

X-RAY BRD02

○ **Birds** have a beak instead of jaws and teeth. Their bones are hollow which makes them light for flying.

○ **Horses'** hooves allow them to travel far over rough ground. Under the hard hoof, they have one bony toe.

○ **Tortoises** protect themselves by curling their backbone to pull their head inside their hard shell.

X-RAY TTS03

X-RAY SNK04

○ **Snakes** don't have legs. They have lots of ribs that allow them to wind their body and slither along.

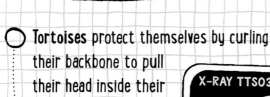

Vets need to know animals inside and out. Match up these animals with their skeletons.

1 Lizard **2** Dog **3** Cat **4** Horse

a)

b)

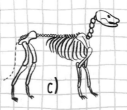
c)

d)

AT THE VET SURGERY

Welcome to the vets' surgery where you will do your on-the-job training. Take a tour, meet the team and find out what happens here.

THE VETERINARY NURSE helps the vet to treat the animals. Each animal needs to be weighed before it is seen by the vet.

PRACTICAL NO: 2

○ tick here

⭐ APPROVED

THE RECEPTIONIST greets people and makes appointments. People can buy toys, leads and food at the reception desk too.

RECEPTION

CHECKLIST

Can you find all your vet's kit at the surgery? Tick the box when you spot each thing.

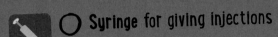 ◯ **Stethoscope** to listen to the heart and chest

 ◯ **Clippers** for cutting long claws

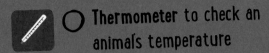 ◯ **Thermometer** to check an animal's temperature

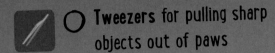 ◯ **Earscope** for looking inside ears

 ◯ **Syringe** for giving injections

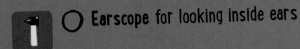 ◯ **Tweezers** for pulling sharp objects out of paws

 VET TIP

Stop germs from spreading! Wash your hands and clean the examination table after each animal patient.

THE VET carefully examines each patient and talks to the owner to find out what the problem is.

EXAMINATION ROOM

ANIMAL TALK

Some pets are scared or grumpy when they visit the vet. Take a class in animal body language to find out how our favourite four-legged friends are feeling.

TELL TALES

Follow the tangled lines to find out what a cat's tail tells you about its mood.

scared ○

friendly ○

angry ○

worried ○

irritated ○

ALL EARS

The position of a cat's ears can tell you a lot.

ALERT	SCARED	ANGRY

○ Ears up and eyes wide ○ Ears flat ○ Ears twisted backwards

DOG TALK DECODER

Dogs use their whole body to show how they are feeling.

Ears up and tail straight = alert

Ears flat and tail down = worried

Tail and head down and shaking body = scared

Bottom up and front legs on the floor = playful

Ears flat and showing teeth = angry

Tail wagging and ears forward = happy

VET'S TIP
Vets can be bitten, kicked or scratched by grumpy animals, so learning their body language is important!

ACTIVITY

How are these pets feeling? Tick the correct word under each picture.

a)
○ worried
○ happy

b)
○ alert
○ playful

c)
○ scared
○ angry

PET CARE

WHAT ANIMALS NEED:

 A comfy home   Fun and games

 Healthy food   Company

BUDGIE FACT FILE

 A large safe cage with a perch in a peaceful place, but where your pet can see what is going on.

 Budgie seeds and pellets, and chopped fresh vegetables and fruit.

 Swings, bells and mirrors, but make sure they have been specially made for pets.

 Budgies can live on their own, but like company.

 VET'S TIP
Your budgie will need exercise outside of its cage every day.

GUINEA PIG FACT FILE

 A safe outside area to run in and a cosy inside space with a bed to snuggle in.

 Water, guinea pig nuggets, soft green hay, safe plants and vegetables.

 Tunnels to run through and boxes filled with hay to hide in.

 Guinea pigs need a guinea pig friend.

 VET'S TIP
Guinea pigs can get colds and chills, so they need regular checks.

Even tiny animals need lots of looking after. Swot up on your pet care facts so that you can give good advice to owners.

CHINCHILLA FACT FILE

 A large indoor cage – they don't like big changes in temperature.

 Chinchilla pellets, fresh hay, and small amounts of fresh vegetables as a treat.

 Platforms, ramps and perches at different heights for climbing fun.

 Can live on their own, but prefer a chinchilla friend to keep them company.

🐾 VET'S TIP
Chinchillas need a sand bath every day to keep their fur shiny and healthy.

GOLDFISH FACT FILE

 The biggest tank or bowl that you have space for.

 Goldfish flakes or pellets. Be careful not to overfeed your fish.

 Tank decorations that provide places to hide and explore.

 Goldfish prefer to have company, though they can live on their own.

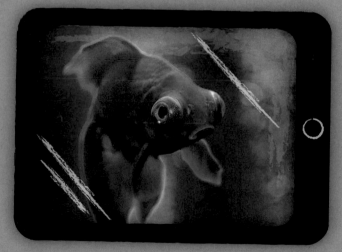

🐾 VET'S TIP
Goldfish need their water changing regularly to stay healthy.

Name of puppy: Jake
Age: 4 months
Favourite toy: ball
Favourite treat: tummy tickle

HEALTH CHECK

It's time to meet your first puppy patient. He needs a full health check before he starts life with his new family.

○ Flea

CREEPY CRITTERS

Pets are a walking feast for lots of minibeasts. Fleas and ticks can live in their fur and feed on their blood. Worms can grow inside pets too. Cats, dogs and rabbits need regular treatment to keep these pests away.

Tick ○

VET SKILL

Tiny fleas are hard to spot, so look for the clues they leave behind:
1. Comb the pet's fur over some kitchen paper.
2. If you find black specks on the paper, add a drop of water.
3. If the specks stain red this is flea poo – full of blood!

Can you spot 3 more fleas hopping about on these pages?

MICRO-CHIPPING

Micro-chipping helps to get lost or stolen pets back with their owners. The vet injects a microchip under the pet's skin. The chip is so small the pet can't feel it. Each microchip has a unique number.

A scanner can detect the microchip. It reads the number which is used to look up the owner's name and address.

VACCINATIONS

Pets need to be vaccinated regularly to stop them catching diseases, and if they travel abroad. The vet injects a small amount of the germ into the animal so their body can learn to fight the disease. This stops the animal from catching it in the future.

VET'S TIP
Have a pot of treats ready to keep pets happy while they are being examined.

PRACTICAL NO: 3
tick here
APPROVED

GOOD GROOMING

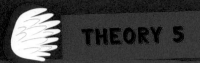

Today the surgery is holding a pampered-pets show. Check out the grooming that is going on behind the scenes. Teeth, coats and claws need to be in top condition!

Cats' and dogs' teeth need cleaning with special toothpaste. Dirty teeth can cause smelly breath and nasty gum infections.

Cats lick themselves clean, but if they swallow too much fur it forms a ball inside them. Brushing removes loose hairs and keeps them healthy.

Long-haired guinea pigs need a regular bath to get rid of tangles and keep their long fur clean.

Some dogs' claws are worn down by walking on pavements. Others need their claws to be clipped.

THEORY NO: 5
tick here
APPROVED

Long-haired pets need their tangles tamed and fur trimmed. If hair flops in their eyes it can cause infections.

ACTIVITY

What an amazing makeover! Can you spot six differences between these two pictures?

BEFORE

AFTER

BLOOD TESTS

A small amount of blood is taken from a vein using a syringe. The blood goes to a laboratory where it is tested to see if there is anything unusual about it.

PRACTICAL 4

WHAT'S WRONG?

PRACTICAL NO. 4
tick here
APPROVED

BODY SCANS

Scans show moving pictures of the inside of the body on a screen. They are used to check the heart and organs, and to see if an animal is pregnant.

Can you spot the broken bone on the x-ray?

X-RAYS

An x-ray machine takes special photographs that show inside an animal's body. They are used to spot injuries and broken bones.

If only pets could talk! For this part of your training you'll need to use special equipment to find out what is wrong with an animal.

VET SKILL

Can you find the matching pair in the x-rays?

a)

b)

c)

d)

TREATMENT TIME

Grab a mask and gown and head for the operating theatre to watch surgeons at work. Then check up on some pets that are on the road to recovery.

OPERATION

CLEAN
Before an operation, surgeons scrub their hands and arms to get rid of germs.

○ Germs cause infections, so everything in the operating theatre must be very clean.

○ The anaesthetic stops the animal from feeling pain during the operation.

SLEEP
The patient breathes in special gas, called anaesthetic, to make it fall sleep.

CHECK
Machines check that the animal's heartbeat and breathing are normal during the operation.

RECOVERY

BANDAGES
Bandages keep wounds clean and stop infections. A hard bandage, called a cast, keeps broken bones in place so that they can mend.

COLLARS
A collar stops the patient from licking its stitches after an operation.

○ This cat has a cast on its broken leg.

BACK HOME

REST
Poorly pets need to rest in a warm, quiet place. Special soft food full of protein, energy and vitamins helps them to recover.

MEDICINES
Pets sometimes need to take pills or medicines to take away pain, or to treat an infection or illness.

○ Hiding a pill inside a treat can trick the pet into eating it.

Can you spot the five differences between the two pictures?

THEORY NO: 6
○ tick here
APPROVED

EXOTIC PETS

Meet some unusual pets for the next part of your training. Whether they are tiny, slimy, scaly or slithery, they all need to be looked after carefully to be happy and healthy.

Most insects eat plants. Some like them rotten!

CREEPY CRAWLIES

Snakes need regular checks for tiny bugs which make their home under the snakes' scales.

BUG BITES

Some exotic pets eat every day, while others only need food once a week. Many amphibians, reptiles and spiders eat live insects!

Pets can get a nasty nip from their living lunch. Uneaten insects should be removed from the tank.

PICK A PET

Can you spot all these exotic pets?

○ Geckos

○ Snakes

○ Lizards

○ Frogs

○ Toads

○ Salamanders

○ Tarantulas

○ Stick insects

○ Giant millipedes

CHILLY LIZARDS

All reptiles need heat to warm their bodies. They get wheezy if their tank is too cold.

THIRSTY SPIDERS

Tarantulas don't drink often, but they do need water or they can die.

FAT FROGS

If they are fed too much these greedy guzzlers can overeat and become ill.

HEALTHY HOMES

Exotic pets need the same things they would have if they lived in the wild. Can you spot these things?

○ hiding holes ○ plants

○ heat lamp ○ water

○ branches ○ rocks

27

ON THE FARM

Wake up! Work starts early down on the farm. There are lots of jobs to do, but before you can treat the animals, you will have to catch them!

JOBS FOR TODAY

Tick the box when you track down each animal.

 ○ **Vaccinate pigs**
Vaccinations stop animals from catching diseases.

 ○ **Treat lamb with sore foot**
Animals can sometimes injure themselves around the farm.

 ○ **Test bull**
Regular checks show whether animals have got any illnesses.

 ○ **Give medicine to turkey**
Many animals need regular medicine to get rid of worms, which grow inside their tummies.

VET'S TIP
Wear overalls and welly boots on the farm. It can be messy and smelly work!

PRACTICAL NO: 5
tick here
APPROVED

VET SKILL

You need to be good at spotting diseases. Farm animals live together in flocks and herds so diseases can spread fast.

This cow has got a serious illness. Find it quickly and count the herd to see how many other cows need checking.

SUNDAY 28th October

GOOD NEWS, EWES!

I visited Gale Farm today to see how many ewes are pregnant. I used my ultrasound scanner which shows a moving picture of the lambs inside the sheep. There are lots of babies on the way. I'll be busy in five months when the ewes give birth!

MONDAY 18th February

IT'S TWINS

I checked a ewe that is expecting twins at Gale Farm. She was a bit weak so I gave her some vitamins.

I told the farmer to give her extra food so that she grows stronger – and the twins inside her grow strong, too.

THEORY 8

A FARM VET'S DIARY

Read Vicky's vet diary to discover how she helps sheep farmers care for their flock – rain or shine, day and night.

MONDAY 1st April

EARLY START

It was wet and cold when I arrived at Gale Farm at 4am, but the lambing shed was warm and dry. I helped a ewe give birth to two lambs. The mother licked them clean and nuzzled them to get them to suckle her milk.

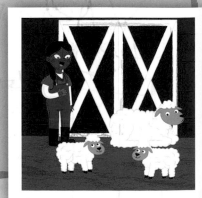

ANIMAL FAMILIES

Match the baby animals with both of their parents.

 FOAL

 CALF

 LAMB

 PIGLET

BABY MILK

All mammals make milk for their babies. The first milk, called colostrum, is packed full of goodness and helps to protect newborns from diseases.

THEORY NO: 8

○⟋ tick here

APPROVED

WEDNESDAY 3rd April

MORE MILK PLEASE!

One of the ewes at Gale Farm did not have enough milk to feed her lamb. This means the lamb must be fed by hand. The farmer needs to give it a bottle every two hours – 8am, 10am, 12pm, 2pm, 4pm, 6pm, 8pm and 10pm!

FRIDAY 10th May

GROWING UP

The lambs at Gale Farm are 6 weeks old now. I gave them their health check and vaccinations to stop them from catching nasty diseases.

Shire horses are tall and very strong. They are used for pulling heavy loads such as carts.

🐾 HOW TALL?

Horses are measured in 'hands'. This is because people used to use the width of their hand to measure them.
One hand = 4 inches.
This shire horse is 64 inches tall.
How many hands is that?
CLUE: divide 64 by 4

Ponies are smaller than horses, with shorter legs and thicker coats. They are tough and strong.

🐾 FRESH HAY

Horses need lots of exercise and plenty of grass and hay to eat. They graze for 18 hours every day!

PRACTICAL 6

Muck in at the stables for a day and learn all about hooves, hands and horses!

Thoroughbred horses are used for racing and show jumping. Like human athletes, they can strain muscles and break bones.

HOOF CARE

Watch out for cracked, painful hooves. Horses' hooves need to be trimmed and filed every six weeks. Stones and dirt need to be scraped out to stop infections, too.

🐾 POO PICKING!

Horses do about eight piles of poo, or manure, every day, It needs to be scooped up or unhealthy germs and bugs can grow.

PRACTICAL NO: 6

tick here

APPROVED

SAFARI PARK

Today you will be treating amazing animals from all over the world! Use this map to find your way around the safari park and complete the jobs on your list below.

REPTILE HOUSE

START HERE

PRIMATE WORLD

JOB LIST

 ○ Examine a poorly **Adelie penguin**

○ Measure the **Nile crocodile**

○ Count the **stick insects**

○ Weigh the **baby rhino**

○ Bandage the tail of a **baboon**

○ Vaccinate the **fruit bats**

KEY

Use this key of the buildings to help you find the animals on your list.

1. TWILIGHT ZONE – owls, aye-ayes and night animals
2. PRIMATE WORLD – monkeys, lemurs and apes
3. BUG JUNGLE – spiders, beetles and other insects
4. SAFARI TRAIL – zebras, giraffes and other African animals
5. OCEAN ODYSSEY – sea birds and seals
6. REPTILE HOUSE – tortoises, snakes and other scaly creatures

TWILIGHT ZONE

This iguana has escaped from its enclosure! Where does it belong?

OCEAN ODYSSEY

BUG JUNGLE

SAFARI TRAIL

ACTIVITY

FINISHED! WELL DONE

Can you find these animals on the map?

◯ Giraffe   ◯ Gorilla   ◯ Lion

◯ Sea lion ◯ Zebra   ◯ Meerkat

PRACTICAL NO: 7
◯ ↰ tick here
APPROVED

SPECIAL TREATMENT

There's no need for medicines today. Head to the animal hospital to discover how poorly pets can feel better with the help of light, water and even wheels!

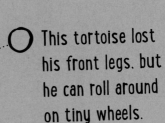

○ This tortoise lost his front legs, but he can roll around on tiny wheels.

SMART PARTS

Some animals may lose a leg in an accident or have it removed if it has a disease. Just like humans, animals can have a false leg fitted to keep them moving.

BODY MATCH

Other body parts are made for animals too. Can you match each of these new body parts to the animal it was made for?

beak   foot   tail

duck

dolphin

parrot

BRIGHT IDEA

Laser treatment shines a beam of special light on an injury. The warm light helps animals to recover from operations and soothes pain. It also helps wounds to heal more quickly.

THEORY NO: 9
tick here
APPROVED

VET'S TIP

Vets AND pets need to wear goggles to protect their eyes from the bright light!

WET WALKIES

Hydrotherapy is treatment in water. It allows old or injured pets to exercise and strengthen their muscles without putting any weight on injured bones and painful joints.

Try to run in the shallow end of a pool. It is hard work to push through the water, but you land softly because the water holds you up.

WORK IN THE WILD

Many different animals around the world are endangered – but adventurous vets can help to keep threatened species fit and healthy so that they survive.

Greenland

Canada

North America

White-backed vulture

South America

Hyacinth macaw

🐾 ENDANGERED ANIMALS

Read up on the four animals under threat below and find out how vets help to make a difference. Can you find each one on the world map?

HAWKSBILL TURTLES

 Where: Florida, USA
Problem: Turtles become ill from eating rubbish dumped in the ocean or get tangled in fishing line.
How can you help? Vets treat sick and injured turtles and release them back into the wild.

LOWLAND GORILLAS

 Where: Rwanda, Africa
Problem: Gorillas get very ill if they catch human illnesses, such as colds, from people.
How can you help? Vets spot poorly gorillas and give them antibiotics.

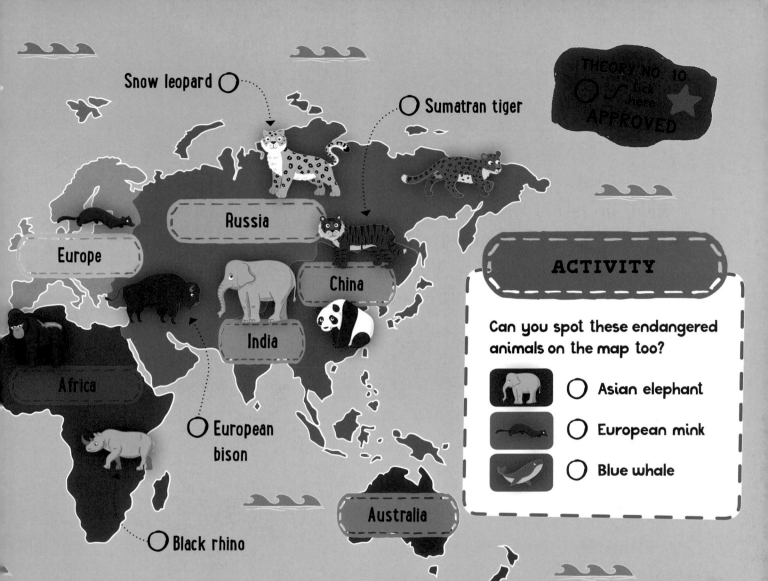

Snow leopard ○

○ Sumatran tiger

Russia

Europe

China

India

Africa

Australia

○ European bison

○ Black rhino

ACTIVITY

Can you spot these endangered animals on the map too?

	○ Asian elephant
	○ European mink
	○ Blue whale

AMUR LEOPARDS

 Where: Russia
Problem: There are only about 70 Amur leopards left in the wild.
How can you help? Vets treat leopards that have diseases to stop them from dying out.

GIANT PANDAS

 Where: China
Problem: Giant pandas are often caught in traps set by hunters to catch deer and other animals.
How can you help? Vets treat their injuries in a special panda hospital.

WILDLIFE RESCUE

Lots of sick, injured or abandoned animals have been brought to this busy animal sanctuary today. Lend a hand and hopefully they can be returned to the wild before too long.

EMERGENCY ROOM

PATIENT: young deer found by the road.

CONDITION: weak and dehydrated with an injured leg.

TREATMENT: attach a drip – a drink given through a tube into a vein. Clean the wound and put a dressing on it.

ISOLATION ROOM

PATIENT: fox cub.

CONDITION: covered in ringworm – a nasty skin infection.

TREATMENT: wash the cub with special shampoo. Keep the cub in a separate room until better. (Ringworm can spread to other animals and humans.)

 VET'S TIP

Watch out! Wild animals can be dangerous. You need to be fully trained to handle them.

A cuddly toy acts as mummy duck for orphans to snuggle!

This seal should weigh 35kg. How many kilograms must it put on?

20kg

ORPHAN WARD

PATIENT: duckling fell down a drain and lost its mother.

CONDITION: cold, shaken and hungry.

TREATMENT: put the duckling under a heat lamp to warm it. Give it food and water and put it with other orphan ducklings.

SEAL POOL

PATIENT: seal found tangled in fishing net.

CONDITION: painful cut on neck and underweight.

TREATMENT: cut away the net and treat the sore skin. Give vitamins and feed with plenty of fish so it can put on lots of blubbery fat.

X-RAY

PATIENT: sick swan.

CONDITION: thin with a droopy neck.

TREATMENT: x-ray shows that this swan has lead poisoning. The dangerous metal needs to be washed out of its tummy.

The swan has swallowed a lead fishing hook.

THEORY 11

JUST THE JOB

ON A FILM SET

<< I work behind the scenes with all sorts of animals, from puppies to penguins! I give the animals a health check and make sure they are safe and happy during filming. I give first aid if there is an animal emergency on set. >>

How many movies or TV shows can you think of that have real animals?

IN THE ARMY

<< I travel all over the world with my job. I look after sniffer dogs and protection dogs that are trained by, and work with, the army. I treat dogs that get ill or injured and make sure that they are well looked after. >>

Phew! Your training is nearly over. Step outside the surgery and meet some vets who work in pretty unusual places.

AT THE AIRPORT

<< I help owners whose pets need to travel by aeroplane. I make sure animals are fit to fly, give vaccinations, and check their pet passports and travel documents. Then I make sure they are safe and comfy in a travel crate, ready for take off.>>

AT THE POLICE STATION

<< Police animals get a lot of injuries because they have a hard job to do. Horses are used to control big crowds and dogs help to solve crimes and catch criminals. It's my job to keep the animals fit and ready for duty. >>

EXAMINATION

Now it's time to see how much you have learned.

1 What kind of animal does an aquatic vet look after?
   a) Reptiles
   b) Birds
   c) Fish

2 What are the bones in the back called?
   a) Verticals
   b) Vertebrae
   c) Veins

3 Which animal needs a sand bath every day?
   a) Goldfish
   b) Cat
   c) Chinchilla

4 How often does a budgie need exercise outside of its cage?
   a) Once a week
   b) Never
   c) Every day

5 What is a syringe used for?
   a) Giving an injection
   b) Looking in the ear
   c) Listening to the heart

6 Which of these is TRUE?
   a) Dogs need their teeth brushed
   b) Cats need their whiskers brushed

7 Which of these bugs lives on pets?
   a) Fleas
   b) Earwigs
   c) Flies

8 Which of these is FALSE?
   a) Guinea pigs should be kept alone
   b) Guinea pigs need to live with a friend

9 What type of animal is a gecko?
   a) Fish
   b) Reptile
   c) Insect

10 Which of these is an exotic pet?
   a) Snake
   b) Ferret
   c) Fox

11 What do pet lizards eat?
   a) Rotten vegetables
   b) Live insects
   c) Tinned meat

12 What is a group of sheep called?
   a) A herd
   b) A bleat
   c) A flock

13 What are horses measured in?
   a) Heads
   b) Hands
   c) Feet

14 What are shire horses used for?
   a) Show jumping
   b) Racing
   c) Pulling heavy loads

15 How often should a horse's hooves be trimmed?
   a) Every six weeks
   b) Every six days
   c) Every six months

VET SCORES

Check your answers at the back of the book and add up your score.

1 to 5 Hsssss! Get back to training and swat up on your animal facts.

6 to 10 Grrrrreat! You are right on track to become a good vet.

11 to 15 Purrrr-fect! You've got what it takes to make a super-vet!

DICTIONARY

VET SPEAK

anaesthetic
A gas or an injection used so that a patient does not feel pain.

antibiotic
A medicine that can destroy harmful bugs in the body.

dehydrated
Not having enough water in the body.

endangered
In danger of being harmed or lost.

infection
A disease in part of the body.

isolation
To be separated from others.

organs
Important parts inside the body that have a special job to do, such as the heart or lungs.

orphan
A child or baby animal whose parents are dead.

micro-chip
A tiny electronic part that can carry information.

parasite
An animal or plant that lives on a different animal or plant and feeds from it.

sanctuary
A place that gives shelter or protection.

skeleton
All the bones inside the body of a person or animal.

species
An animal that belongs to a set of animals which often look the same.

vaccination
A special treatment that stops a person or animal from catching a disease.

VET ACADEMY

WELL DONE!

You made it through your vet training.

Name...

FULLY QUALIFIED

VET

ANSWERS

Page 6
The odd one out is the guinea pig because it does not have a bandage.

Page 10

- Skull
- Vertebrae
- Ribs

a) whale, b) bat, c) monkey, d) frog.

Page 11
1b, 2c, 3d, 4a.

Page 12
The things to find are circled below:

Page 14

angry   friendly   scared

worried   irritated

Page 15
a = happy, b = alert, c = scared.

Page 18-19

Page 21

Page 23

The broken bone is circled right:

a and d = matching pair

Page 25
The differences to find are circled right:

Page 26-27
The pets to spot art circled below in red. The other items are circled in blue:

Page 28-29
The animals to spot are circled below in red. The sick cow is circled in blue:

Page 31
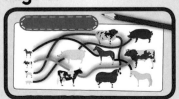

Page 32
The horse is 16 hands.

Page 32-33
The wheelbarrow is circled below:

Page 34-35
Adelie penguin = Ocean Odyssey
Nile crocodile = Reptile House
Stick insects = Bug Jungle
Baby rhino = Safari Trail
Baboon = Primate World
Fruit bats = Twilight Zone

The iguana belongs in the Reptile House.

Page 36

Page 38-39

Page 41
The seal must put on 15kg.

Page 44-45
1 = c; 2 = b; 3 = c; 4 = c; 5 = a;
6 = a; 7 = a; 8 = b; 9 = b; 10 = a;
11 = b; 12 = c; 13 = b; 14 = c; 15 = a.